Acadia

American Samoa

Arches

Badlands

Big Bend

Black Canyon

Bryce Canyon

Canyonlands

Capitol Reef

Carlsbad Caverns

Channel Islands

Congaree

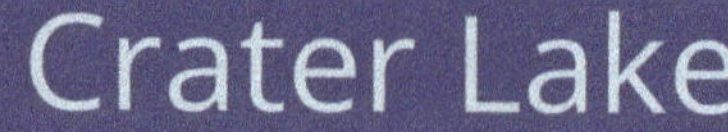

Crater Lake

Cuyahoga Valley

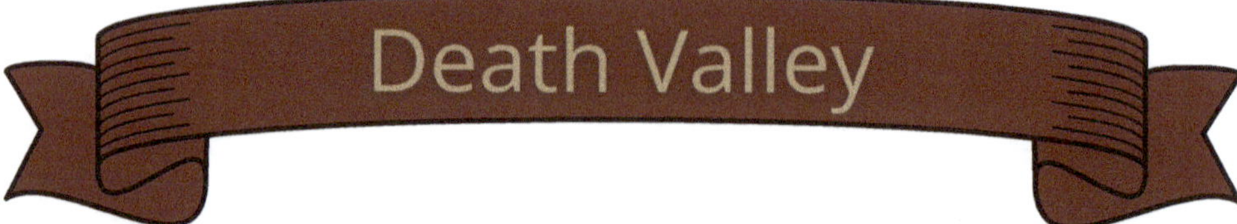
Death Valley

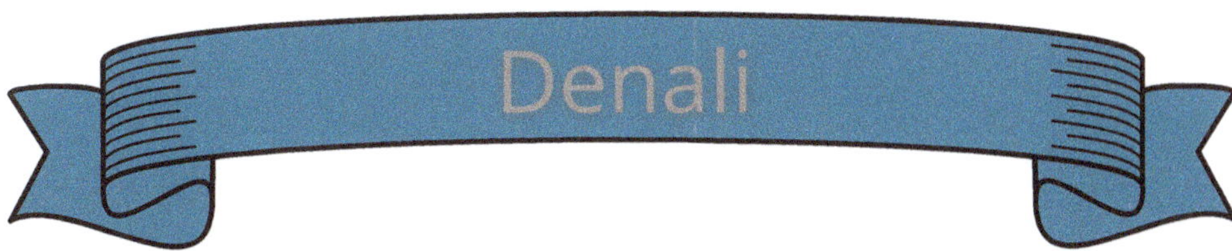

Denali

Dry Tortugas

Everglades

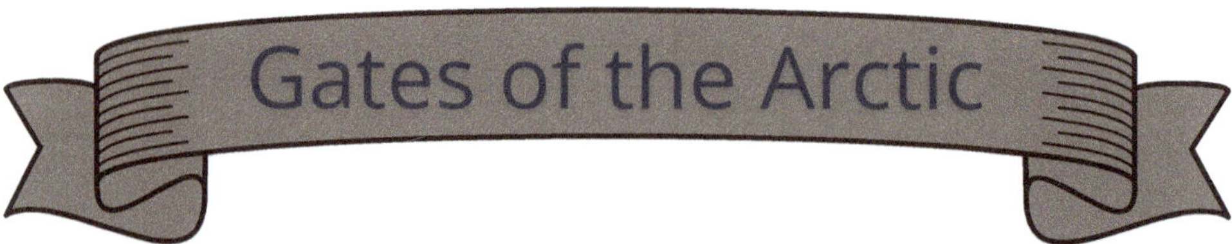

Gates of the Arctic

Glacier

Glacier Bay

Grand Canyon

Grand Teton

Great Basin

Great Sand Dunes

Great Smoky Mountains

Guadalupe Mountains

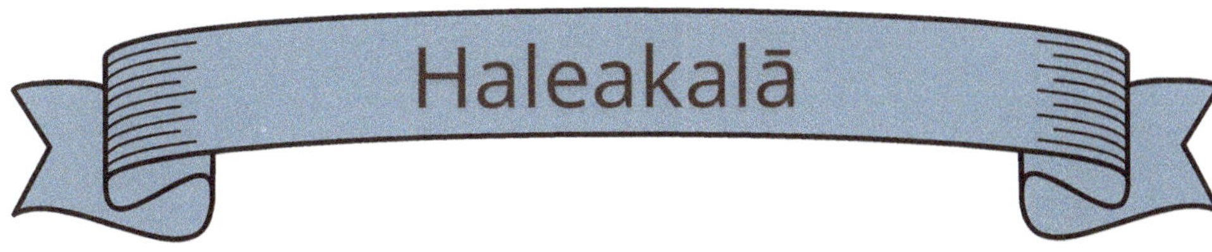

Haleakalā

Hawai'i Volcanoes

Hot Springs

Indiana Dunes

Joshua Tree

Katmai

Kenai Fjords

Kings Canyon

Kobuk Valley

Lake Clark

Lassen Volcanic

Mammoth Cave

Mesa Verde

Mount Rainier

New River Gorge

North Cascades

Olympic National Park

Petrified Forest

Pinnacles

Redwood

Rocky Mountain

Saguaro

Sequoia

Shenandoah

Theodore Roosevelt

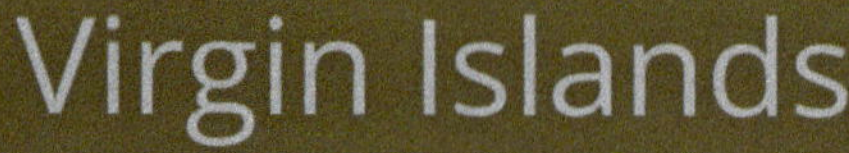

Virgin Islands

Voyageur

White Sands

Wind Cave

Wrangell–St. Elias

Yellowstone

Yosemite

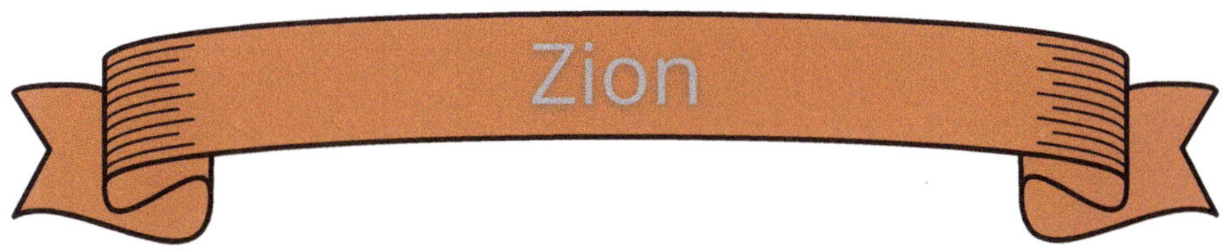
Zion

Acknowledgement

Page No. I Author/s I Title I Source I License

American Samoa	U.S. Department of the Interior	Si'u Point Trail, Ta'u Island, National Park of American Samoa	https://www.flickr.com/photos/usinterior/9109117816/	Attribution-ShareAlike 2.0 Generic (CC BY-SA 2.0)
Kings Canyon	James OBrien II	Kings Canyon August 2012 016	https://www.flickr.com/photos/jpo2/7772598506/	Attribution 2.0 Generic (CC BY 2.0)
Petrified Forest	Kevin Dooley	Petrified Forest 2021	https://www.flickr.com/photos/pagedooley/51481333270/	Attribution 2.0 Generic (CC BY 2.0)
Voyageur National Park	Fighting Irish 1977	Voyageur National Park (Crane Lake)	https://www.flickr.com/photos/globaltrotters/36550012290/	Attribution 2.0 Generic (CC BY 2.0)
White Sands	John Fowler	White Sands	https://www.flickr.com/photos/snowpeak/4814702565/	Attribution 2.0 Generic (CC BY 2.0)